Up & Running
with Windows™ 3.0

Gabriele Wentges

SYBEX ®

San Francisco • Paris • Düsseldorf • Soest

Acquisitions Editor: Dianne King
Translator: Larry Childs
Revisor: Avon Murphy
Editor: Richard Mills
Technical Editor: Dan Tauber
Word Processor: Deborah Maizels
Book Designer: Elke Hermanowski
Icon Designer: Helen Bruno
Screen Graphics: Delia Brown
Desktop Publishing Production: Helen Bruno
Proofreader: R. M. Holmes
Indexer: Nancy Anderman Guenther
Cover Designer: Archer Design

SYBEX is a registered trademark of SYBEX, Inc.

TRADEMARKS: SYBEX has attempted throughout this book to distinguish proprietary trademarks from descriptive terms by following the capitalization style used by the manufacturer.

SYBEX is not affiliated with any manufacturer.

Every effort has been made to supply complete and accurate information. However, SYBEX assumes no responsibility for its use, nor for any infringement of the intellectual property rights of third parties which would result from such use.

Authorized translation from German Language Edition.
Original copyright © SYBEX-Verlag GmbH 1989.
Translation © SYBEX Inc. 1990.

Copyright © 1990 SYBEX Inc., 2021 Challenger Drive, Alameda, CA 94501. World rights reserved. No part of this publication may be stored in a retrieval system, transmitted, or reproduced in any way, including but not limited to photocopy, photograph, magnetic or other record, without the prior agreement and written permission of the publisher.

Library of Congress Card Number: 90-70371
ISBN: 0-89588-711-8

Manufactured in the United States of America
10 9 '

Up & Running

Let's say that you are comfortable with your PC. You know the basic functions of word processing, spreadsheets, and database management. In short, you are a committed and eager PC user who would like to gain familiarity with several popular programs as quickly as possible. The Up & Running series of books from SYBEX has been developed for you.

Who this book is for

This clearly structured guide shows you in 20 steps what the product can do, how you make it work, and how soon you can achieve practical results.

What this book provides

Your Up & Running book thus satisfies two needs: It describes the program's capabilities, and it lets you quickly get acquainted with the program's operation. This provides valuable help for a purchase decision. You also receive a 20-step basic course that provides a solid foundation in the program—even if you're a beginner with scant prior knowledge.

The benefits are plain to see. First, you will invest in software that meets your needs, because, thanks to the appropriate Up & Running book, you will know the program's features and limitations. Second, once you purchase the product, you can skip the instruction manual and learn the basics of the program by following the 20 steps.

We have structured the Up & Running books so that the busy user spends little time studying documentation and the beginner is not burdened with unnecessary text.

Structure of the book

A clock shows your work time for each step. This indicates how much time you can expect to spend on each step with your computer.

Required time

 **Clock**

Naturally, you'll need much less time if you only read through the steps rather than carrying them out at your computer. You can also save some time by scanning the short notes in the margins to find the most important sections within a step.

Three symbols are used to highlight points of special note. These symbols and their meanings are shown below:

Symbols

Action

Tip

Warning

An Up & Running book cannot, of course, replace a book or manual containing advanced applications. However, you will get the information needed to put the program to practical use and to learn its basic functions.

Contents   The first step explains how to install Windows 3.0. Steps 2 and 3 acquaint you with the Windows user interface and screen. The remaining steps teach you how to load and run applications, how to manipulate windows, how to use all of Windows' resident applications, and how to customize the program.

An Up & Running book will save you time and money.

SYBEX is very interested in your reaction to the Up & Running series. Your opinions and suggestions will help all of our readers, including yourself.

Preface

Windows is the computer cockpit from which you control all your computer's capabilities with the push of a button. Like the pilot of a modern, sophisticated aircraft, you are guided quickly through Windows' many functions by graphic symbols.

Because of the forward-thinking Windows design, you have much the same style of interface as found in OS/2 Presentation Manager and Unix's X Window. You can switch easily between applications and between documents to control all your work.

Windows also provides you with electronic versions of tools like the typical office calendar, Rolodex, and note pad. You use these applications in the same intuitive way as you use Windows itself.

With only a little extra effort, you can master high-powered Windows-based programs for desktop publishing, spreadsheets, and word processing, such as PageMaker, Excel, and Word.

After giving you a brief overview of Windows, this book quickly teaches you the basics of the Windows applications. You then learn ways to increase your computing power. With its emphasis on essentials and its practice-oriented instructions, this book will have you using Windows for your daily work in no time.

I hope that this book will spare you time-consuming study of the extensive documentation, and I wish you fun and success with "windowing."

Gabriele Wentges
June 1990

Table of Contents

Before you begin using Windows, you must install and customize the program according to your computer's configuration. You use the Setup program, which installs Windows in a dialogue with you.

Equipment Requirements

Check with your dealer or with Microsoft to make sure that Windows is equipped to work with your hardware and software.

Windows 3.0 runs on a wide range of computers, including IBM PC/ATs and compatibles, 80386- and 80486-based systems, and PS/2 systems.

Computer

You should have a graphics card that is Hercules-, EGA-, or VGA-compatible; I don't recommend using a CGA card. Windows also supports a number of full-page-display monitors.

Graphics card and monitor

You need a hard disk with at least 6MB of free space. You also need at least one high-density floppy-disk drive. I don't recommend using low-density disk drives.

Disk drives

You can use almost any printer that supports paint fonts and graphics.

Printer

You need MS-DOS or PC-DOS 3.1 or higher to run Windows.

DOS

Making Backup Copies

Make copies of the Windows disks before installing them. If you have two disk drives, you can create a backup copy by typing this command:

`DISKCOPY A: B:`

If you have only one drive, type this command:

`DISKCOPY A: A:`

You are then asked to exchange the disk in drive A with another one. Follow the directions on the screen until all the Windows disks have been copied.

Installing Windows

To install Windows, insert the Windows disk containing the Setup program (Disk 1) in drive A.

You must use the Setup program. Never try to copy Windows files directly onto your hard disk.

Start the installation by typing

`SETUP`

Press Enter. Setup "reads" your system so that it can offer logical recommendations as you choose various settings. On-screen prompts guide you through the installation process, helping you insert the proper disks and set up Windows to work properly with your hardware and software.

Getting
help

At most points in the process, you can press F1 to read Help screens like those you find in Windows itself. You can press F3 to get out of Setup without completing the installation.

At the first options screen, press Enter to continue. Setup proposes a logical choice for a Windows directory to create. You should type in a different directory name if the default choice doesn't meet your needs. If Setup recommends

C:\WINDOWS, for example, and you want to install Windows on a D drive, type

`D:\WINDOWS`

Press Enter when the directory name appears as you want it.

Setup goes on to make usually accurate recommendations for your computer system, monitor, mouse, keyboard type and layout, language, and network. To change a setting, move to the appropriate selection by pressing the appropriate arrow key, press Enter to see alternatives, and make the new selection.

You're also asked whether you want to set up printers, set up applications already installed on your hard disks, and read on-line documents. It's usually best to confirm these choices.

As Setup copies files to your Windows directory, you see bar graphs indicating the percentage of files copied. Small pictographs (called icons) appear on some screens, indicating that standard Windows applications are loading.

Next, you see three options for making the necessary changes in your CONFIG.SYS and AUTOEXEC.BAT files. Unless you have a definite reason to do otherwise, you should elect to have these files modified automatically.

A list of supported printers appears. Highlight the one you are using and press Enter. You may want to include one printer under two selections on this list, if that printer can be run under two modes (for example, Epson- and HP-compatible).

If your printer is not included on the list of supported devices, you must install the printer driver available from the printer manufacturer. You can also define additional printers later by using the Windows Control Panel (see Step 13).

Next, Setup searches your hard drives for applications that can be started easily from within Windows. One box on the screen contains application names. Simply select Add (or Add All), and the applications' names appear in the Added box.

Finally, you see Windows 3.0 Release Notes. After exiting Setup, you must restart Windows to put the installation options you selected into effect. If you later decide to modify your basic hardware and software settings, you can rerun Setup, either inside or outside Windows.

Step 2
The User Interface

In this step, you learn how the user interface helps you get around Windows easily.

A user interface is a combination of tools that streamline your work and shield you from the complexity of your computer's system operation. The Windows interface combines screen display, user controls, and online help.

The Screen Display

You can find your way around quickly in Windows because of its highly graphic orientation. Applications and documents appear in windows, which are separate areas on your screen set off by their own borders. Applications can also appear as icons, which are small pictorial representations of applications whose windows are closed.

User Controls

You can open, close, move, and change the size of the windows themselves. You can cut or copy work from one application and paste it into another. You can also run a number of applications on your screen simultaneously.

Varied controls make it easy to issue such commands. You can use either your mouse or your keyboard to select on-screen commands, pull down menus, press buttons, and fill in dialog boxes.

Online Help

Windows provides excellent online help. If you need explanations while working, choose the Help command or press F1. The same command gives you access to the online tutorial.

With this kind of user interface, Windows is anything but intimidating.

This step acquaints you with the very heart of Windows, the windows themselves. Using windows is an efficient way to represent the working of applications on the screen.

All the application windows are constructed in an identical manner from one unified set of structural elements. Not all the elements are present in every Windows application, and a few elements vary slightly from application to application. It will be enough for now, however, if you learn the overall construction of a typical window and the functions of its individual elements.

Let's look, for example, at a screen that shows the clear structuring of Windows applications (see Figure 3.1). Individual

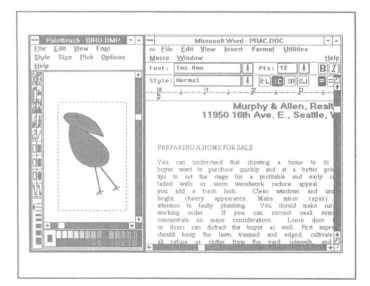

Figure 3.1: Application windows

windows can be stacked on top of one another. This layered approach allows you to copy individual drawings from one window into another.

Elements of a Window

The Windows screen can contain one or more windows. (The maximum number depends mainly on which applications you are running.) Figure 3.2 illustrates the typical layout of a Windows screen. (The circled numbers in the figure correspond to the numbers next to the explanations below.)

1. The *window border* is part of the window, even when the window takes up the entire screen, and serves as the window's boundary.

2. The icon at the corner of the border is used to change the size of the window (it does not show up in all windows).

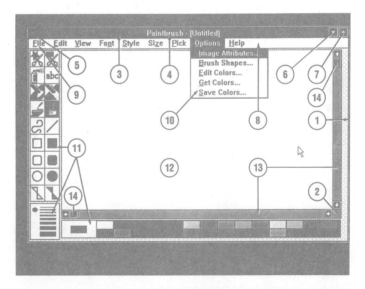

Figure 3.2: Layout of a Windows application screen

3. The *title bar* contains the name of the window.

4. The name of the application and document identifies the window.

5. The *Control-menu box* calls up the following options: Restore, Move, Size, Minimize, Maximize, Close, and Switch To. Other options may appear on other applications' Control menus.

6. The *Minimize box* (down arrow) reduces the window to an icon, without ending the application.

7. The *Maximize box* (up arrow) makes the window fill the entire screen. When a window has been maximized, the box changes to the Restore box.

8. The *menu bar* is used to choose application menus and to call up Help functions. The menus available depend on the application you are using. As a rule, however, the File, Edit, and Help menus are always available.

9. The *File menu* contains such options as New, Open, Save, and Exit, which allow you to perform various operations on your files. The options vary from application to application.

10. A *pull-down menu* drops down to reveal options you can select with the keyboard or with the mouse. This menu usually appears directly under the menu item to which it belongs.

11. Three tools menus in Figure 3.2 contain icons that graphically represent frequently used functions as pictographs. (These menus do not appear in every Windows application.)

12. This is an open *work space* in which text, graphics, and other objects to be edited can be shown, altered, and moved. In graphics applications, the objects may either partly or completely fill up the work space, which is also called the drawing area or the layout area.

13. The horizontal and vertical *scroll bars* position the visible portions of objects that project horizontally or vertically beyond the area of the window.

14. The highlighted squares on the scroll bars, called *scroll boxes,* move along the bars and show the relative position of the visible portion of the object.

Example of an Application Window

Reversi

The game Reversi, included in your Windows package, offers a simple example of a window (see Figure 3.3). The object to be worked on is the Reversi playing board, along with the game to be placed on it. The board is found in the middle of the work space and is surrounded by a border. The name Reversi appears in the title bar. To the left is the Control-menu box, and to the right are the Minimize and Maximize icons.

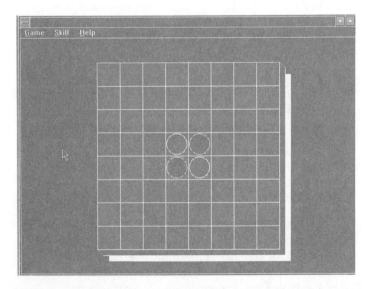

Figure 3.3: Application window for Reversi

The menu bar offers the choices Game, Skill, and Help. From this bar, the pull-down Game menu has the options Hint, Pass, New, and Exit. The pull-down Skill menu offers the Beginner, Novice, Expert, and Master levels of difficulty. The pull-down Help menu offers the options Index, Keyboard, Commands, Playing the Game, Rules, Using Help, and About Reversi.

Dialog Boxes

When you select the option About Reversi on the Game menu, a dialog box with version and copyright information is superimposed on the window (see Figure 3.4).

Dialog boxes are windowlike areas that you cannot alter. They usually contain short messages and ask you to respond to a multiple-choice option list. In the example in Figure 3.4,

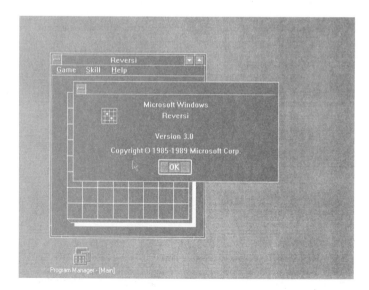

Figure 3.4: Dialog box in Reversi

your only possible answer is OK, but other questions could also take the answers Yes, No, or Cancel.

A dialog box is an important part of an application window, and the questions in them must be answered before you can do more work in the window. Dialog boxes appear primarily in error situations or when a large number of settings are necessary before you can begin a certain phase of editing.

Subwindows

The Microsoft Excel application, a spreadsheet program, makes extensive use of subwindows (see Figure 3.5). These allow the simultaneous display of different spreadsheet areas for large-scale calculations, as well as the display of results and notes on individual formulas and data fields.

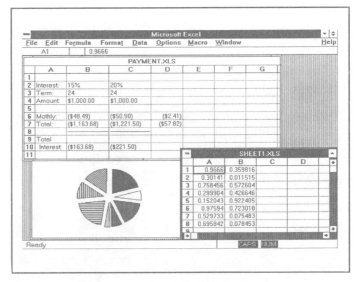

Figure 3.5: Application window with subwindows

In Figure 3.5, three subwindows are displayed, each containing a different document. The spreadsheet subwindow in the lower-right corner shows two columns of data. This same data is displayed in a pie-chart subwindow on the left side. Along the top of the screen is another spreadsheet subwindow that compares the payments on a loan at two interest rates. The value of the currently selected cell (A1 of spreadsheet SHEET1.XLS) is displayed in the edit bar beneath Excel's menu bar.

Step 4

Starting and Ending

Now that you're comfortable with the terminology of the Windows user interface, we'll begin looking at practical applications. First, you'll learn how to start and end Windows and Windows applications.

Starting Windows

You should have installed Windows on a hard disk and changed the AUTOEXEC.BAT file so that Windows can be started with the WIN command. (As I mentioned in Step 1, you'll find it easier to let Setup automatically change this file.)

In the exercises that follow in this book, I'll represent a sequence of keys for you to press by separating the key names with a space, for example, F7 N. This sequence means to press the F7 key, then press the letter N.

Key sequence

I'll represent two keys for you to press at the same time by putting a hyphen between them, for example, Alt-F4. This combination means to press the function key F4 while holding down the Alt key.

Key combination

Follow these steps to start Windows:

1. Turn on your PC. Enter the date and time if prompted to do so. Your computer will display a prompt like *C>*.

2. At the prompt, type the command to start Windows. Type

   WIN

   and press Enter. Windows determines the best mode to run in based on the system you have; however, you can tell Windows which mode to run in, if you like. If you're going to use software written for earlier versions of Windows, you must run Windows in *real* mode. Type

`WIN/R`

and press Enter. An 80386 or 80486 computer performs better when you start the program in *standard* or in *386 enhanced* mode. Type either of the following:

`WIN/S`

or

`WIN/3`

Press Enter.

3. The Windows title screen soon appears. Windows starts with the Program Manager window open. The Program Manager helps you organize the applications that you run in Windows.

Starting an Application Directly

There are several ways you can start an application directly:

1. Use the mouse or the arrow keys to select the name of the application from inside the Program Manager (see Step 7) or the File Manager (see Step 8).

2. At the DOS prompt (usually *C>*), enter the proper commands for Windows and the application. The Write application (Windows' resident word processor), for example, opens inside its own window after you enter

`WIN WRITE`

Starting an Application Indirectly

Windows also offers the option of starting an application indirectly by loading a file that has been created with that application. This method saves you several extra steps.

Assume, for instance, that you've saved a Write document as LETTER4.WRI. You begin automatically in the document after entering

```
WIN WRITE LETTER4
```

There are several powerful but more complicated options for starting applications. They involve the modification of files. These options are described in Step 19 and Step 20.

Ending an Application

You exit all Windows applications in basically the same way. In contrast, you exit non-Windows applications (such as WordPerfect) using the procedures normally used in those individual applications.

Let's assume you've finished working on the Write document LETTER4.WRI.

1. Pull down the File menu (or press Alt-F).

2. Select Exit. If you've modified the letter, a dialog box asks whether you want to save the changes. (If this were a new document, you'd also type a file name into the File Save As text box.) The Write window closes.

Exiting Windows

Follow these steps to exit Windows:

1. Close any open windows before leaving Windows. The easiest way to do this is to click on each active window's Control-menu box (or press Alt-F4).

2. A dialog box appears for each window, asking for confirmation of your intention to exit. Make sure OK is highlighted and press Enter each time.

3. Windows alerts you if any of the applications contain files that have been changed but not saved.

4. Exit the Program Manager; you are out of Windows.

In the next step, you'll learn how to manipulate the location and the size of windows on the screen.

Step 5
Managing Windows

15

In this step you learn about how you can control the individual windows themselves. You can alter their size and placement, go in and out of them, and work simultaneously on different applications. You can not only display several document windows within the same application but also display several different application windows at the same time.

Sizing Windows

You can make a window occupy the entire screen, make it fill only a portion of the screen, or reduce it to an icon. The example in Figure 5.1 shows the window for the Clock application on an otherwise empty screen. You can expand or compress a window by dragging the corner icons or window borders with the mouse or by using the arrow keys.

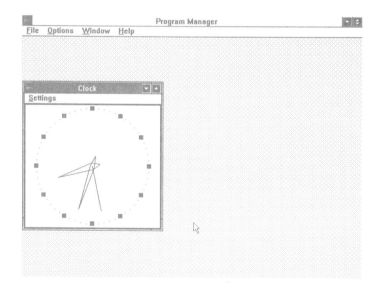

Figure 5.1: The Clock application

Maximizing Windows

You can expand the Clock window to fill the entire area of the screen by maximizing the window (see Figure 5.2). To do so, use the mouse to click on the Maximize box or use the arrow keys to select Maximize on the Control menu.

Minimizing Windows

You follow the same general steps to make a window smaller. When you select Minimize, the Clock window closes and disappears. An icon representing the Clock appears in the lower-left corner of the screen (see Figure 5.3). Icons can be moved around on the screen just like windows.

You can later select the Clock icon and reopen its window. From its Control menu, you can either select Restore to return it to its original size or select Maximize to enlarge it.

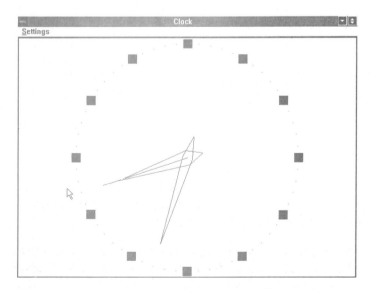

Figure 5.2: The Clock application as a full screen

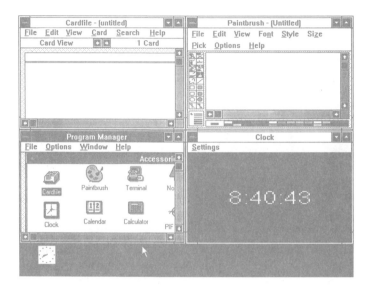

Figure 5.3: Application windows and Clock icon

Opening Multiple Windows

More than one window at a time can appear on the Windows screen. The maximum number of windows you can open depends on available memory in your computer. Figure 5.3 shows several windows visible simultaneously.

When there are several open windows on the screen, you have to know which window you can use; only one window at a time is active. This window can carry on a dialogue with you, send messages, display results, and receive commands. It is clearly designated by a dark background on its title bar. You can activate a specific window by using the mouse to click on it or by pressing the appropriate key.

Making a window active

There are two ways you can arrange multiple open windows. You can pull down the Window menu and choose to make the

Arranging windows

windows cascade, or pile on top of one another. The top window is always the active one. You can also choose the tiling option, in which the windows line up side by side. (This is how the windows are arranged in Figure 5.3.) With this arrangement, you can easily look at and move between two or more documents or applications simultaneously.

Moving windows

You can also move a window around on the screen by dragging its title bar with the mouse or by using the arrow keys. If windows overlap, the active one always appears in the foreground. You can get to covered windows by leafing through them using keyboard commands, or you can diminish the size of or remove altogether the windows on top.

The surface on which windows can be moved around is greater than what is displayed on the Windows screen. You can move windows horizontally and vertically off the screen.

Moving data between windows

A prime benefit of Windows is the ease with which you can move information quickly between windows. You can use the Copy, Cut, and Paste commands (located on the Edit menu of most applications) to place material from one window in another window.

Step 6
Mouse and Keyboard

This step introduces you to the two basic ways to issue commands in Windows: using the mouse and using the keyboard. At first you'll probably find using the mouse to be the most comfortable way to control Windows. But you'll also find the keyboard easy to work with, especially after a little practice.

You'll learn how to perform these basic operations with both the mouse and the keyboard:

- Making a window active
- Changing a window's size
- Moving a window
- Scrolling a window's contents
- Working with files
- Working with multiple windows
- Working with active windows
- Ending your session

Mouse Functions

You can run Windows using the left mouse button and only five mouse control functions.

The following is a list of general mouse-control functions. Some applications won't utilize all these functions.

1. *Pointing:* Move the mouse on the pad or your desktop so that the diagonal arrow points to an object on the Windows screen.

2. *Selecting or clicking:* Point to an object, and press the left button.

3. *Choosing or double clicking:* Point to an object, and press the left button twice.

4. *Dragging:* While holding the left button down, move the pointer over a list, over sections of text, or over individual graphic objects.

5. *Marking:* Click on the selection bar, or drag it over a list or sections of text, or stretch a selection area over part of a graphic object by holding the left button down (group selection).

Mouse Objects

The objects that can be addressed by the mouse are window elements that were introduced to you in Step 3:

- Window borders
- Corner icons
- Title bar
- Control-menu box
- Minimize box
- Maximize box
- Menu names in the menu bar
- Highlighted menu options
- Icon graphics in a tools menu
- Work spaces
- Objects and symbols in work areas
- Scroll boxes and arrows in a scroll bar
- Page icons

You can also click on text entries in lists, text boxes, command buttons in dialog boxes, and letter symbols.

Keyboard Functions

Like mouse operations, keyboard operations are generally the same from one Windows application to another. Single-key shortcuts often replace several mouse maneuvers.

You can access every menu option whose name contains an underlined letter by pressing that letter on the keyboard. However, to access menu names in the menu bar, you must also press the Alt key.

An example of a shortcut is activating a pull-down menu within a window. In the Program Manager window, for example, you can reach the

- File menu by pressing Alt-F

- Options menu by pressing Alt-O

- Window menu by pressing Alt-W

- Help menu by pressing Alt-H

You can access a window's Control menu by pressing Alt-spacebar if you're in an application window, or Alt-hyphen if you're in a document window.

Running Windows Efficiently

You will find that it may not be best or even possible to use your mouse in every situation. In some cases, you may find it most practical to use a combination of keyboard commands and mouse functions or just the keyboard commands alone.

Manipulating Windows

Start Windows, as described in Step 4. You begin at the open Program Manager window. Let's practice some basic operations with both the mouse and the keyboard.

Changing Window Size with the Mouse

1. Point to the upper-left corner of the Program Manager window; the pointer changes to a two-headed arrow.

2. Hold down the left button, and drag the pointer to different areas of the screen without releasing the button. Notice how the window's borders expand and contract.

3. Release the button when the pointer is anywhere on the screen but where it began. The window is now a different size.

Changing Window Size with the Keyboard

1. Open the Program Manager window's Control menu. Since you're in an application window, you have to press Alt-spacebar.

2. Select Size. You can press S or use ↓ to highlight Size and press Enter. A four-pointed cursor appears.

3. Press the arrow keys to change the window's size. Press Enter when you're finished.

Moving a Window with the Mouse

Drag the title bar upward and to the right so that the active window is placed precisely in the upper right-hand corner of the Windows screen.

Moving a Window with the Keyboard

1. Open the Control menu.

2. Select Move. You can press M or use ↓ to highlight Move and press Enter.

3. Use the arrow keys to relocate the window. Press Enter.

Scrolling the Contents of a Window

Different applications and documents present different scroll bars on the right and bottom sides of their windows. The window in Figure 6.1 can only be scrolled horizontally, so you see only a bottom scroll bar.

With the mouse, you drag the pointer along the scroll bar to view more program group icons. With the keyboard, you

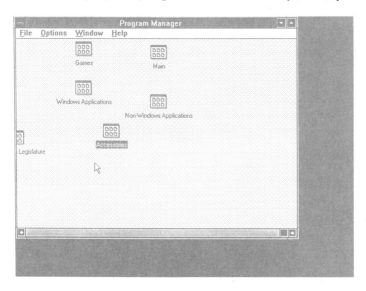

Figure 6.1: Scrolling a window

press Ctrl-F6 (or Ctrl-Tab) to move the highlight from icon to icon.

Working with Files

Windows commands make it easy to perform many file operations. For the following exercises, start at the open Program Manager window.

Opening a File with the Mouse

1. Double-click on the Accessories icon to open the Accessories program group.

2. Double-click on the Write icon (representing the Write application). In a few seconds, the Write window opens.

3. Click on the File menu name. This menu contains all the necessary commands for working with files. Besides the Control menu, this is the most important menu in Windows; it is used in almost all applications.

4. Click on the menu option Open.

5. Select any file from the directory list in the dialog box. Open it by double-clicking on it.

Opening a File with the Keyboard

1. Press Ctrl-F6 (or Ctrl-Tab) until the Accessories icon is highlighted. Press Enter.

2. Move the highlight to the Write icon by using the arrow keys and press Enter.

3. Press Alt-F to open the File menu.

4. Press O or use the arrow keys to highlight Open. Press Enter.

5. Use Tab and the arrow keys to highlight any file name. Press Enter.

Saving a File

After you make changes to a file, you can save them.

Saving a File with the Mouse

1. Click on the Save option in the File menu. Any changes you have made are written to the file. The previous contents of the file are erased.

2. If you don't want the original text to be written over, you can save the changed text under a different name. To do this, click on the Save As option on the File menu.

Changing a file name

3. A dialog box appears, and you can enter the new name. When you type the first letter, the old name is automatically deleted. When you're done, click on the OK command button. (If you omit the file-name extension, Write uses .WRI by default.)

If you make a mistake while entering the new name, you can cancel it and start over by pressing Esc.

Saving a File with the Keyboard

Press Alt-F to open the File menu. Press S or highlight Save and press Enter.

Printing a File

1. Pull down the File menu.

2. Select Print.

3. Select OK in the dialog box that pops up. The dialog box disappears by itself.

Working with Multiple Windows

For the following exercises, keep the Write window active. Move and, if necessary, resize it so that it occupies roughly the right two-thirds of your screen.

Working with Active Windows Using the Mouse

1. Click on the File Manager icon in the Main program group.

2. Click on the Directory Tree window containing the file name WRITE.EXE. The directory window becomes active again. The title bar of the Write window turns gray, signifying that the window is no longer active.

3. Scroll through the directory list by repeatedly clicking on the right scroll arrow or by dragging along the scroll bar of the active window.

4. Double-click on the Clock icon in the Accessories program group. The Clock window will overlap the Write window (see Figure 6.2).

5. Click on the Write window so it becomes active again. It now overlaps the Clock window. If the window you want to make active is hidden, click on the desktop (anywhere on the Windows screen) to open a Task List. Double-click on the window name.

Ending the application

6. End the Write application by clicking on the Control-menu box and then on the menu option Close. If you've made any changes to the file, you are asked to save them before the Write application is closed.

7. To change the Clock into an icon, click on the Mini-mize box, the down arrow to the right of the title bar.

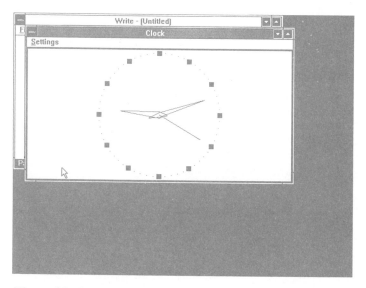

Figure 6.2: Overlapping windows

Working with Active Windows Using the Keyboard

1. Open the Task List. There are two ways to do this:

   • Press Alt-spacebar to open the Write window's Control menu, then select Switch To.

   • Press Ctrl-Esc.

2. From the Task List, choose the name of the directory window. Press Enter. This window becomes active.

3. Use the keyboard skills you've learned to do the following:

   • Open the Clock window.

   • Switch between windows.

   • Close the application.

   • Minimize the Clock.

Ending Windows with the Mouse

1. Click on the Program Manager icon.

2. Select the Exit option.

3. Confirm your selection by clicking on the OK command button.

4. If the Save Changes box in the Exit dialog box contains an *X*, all changes will be saved in your unclosed windows. Toggle this box on and off.

Ending Windows with the Keyboard

1. Press Alt-spacebar to make the Program Manager active.

2. Select Close.

3. Confirm your desire to exit by pressing Enter.

4. If you want to save any changes, move to the Save Changes box by pressing Tab.

5. Press the spacebar to toggle the box on and off.

Step 7
The Program Manager

In this step you'll learn how to use Program Manager. With this controller, you select graphic icons to open windows and load applications.

What Program Manager Can Do

Program Manager (see Figure 7.1) comes up on the screen automatically when you start Windows, unless you've made changes that let a particular Windows application come up instead.

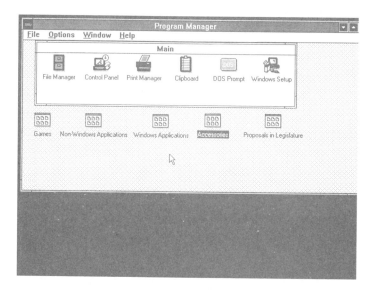

Figure 7.1: The Program Manager

You can greatly improve your working efficiency with Program Manager in two ways:

- You can use Program Manager's organizational power to arrange your applications into groups that make sense for your work habits.

- You can use Program Manager's representation of applications as icons to start programs quickly, without having to type their names.

Organizing Your Work

The key to truly efficient work in Windows is the way you arrange the applications that you use most often.

With Windows running, select Accessories within Program Manager. Open Notepad by double-clicking on its icon or by moving the highlight onto it with the arrow keys and pressing Enter. Select Open on the File menu, type PROGMAN.INI in the Filename box, and press OK.

One section will show how you've set up your groups. You might see, for instance,

Group1=D:\WINDOWS\ACCESSOR.GRP

Group2=D:\WINDOWS\GAMES.GRP

Group3=D:\WINDOWS\MAIN.GRP

Group4=D:\WINDOWS\WINDOWSA.GRP

These entries indicate that you have four groups named Accessories, Games, Main, and Windows Applications.

Within Program Manager, you can easily organize your work by establishing and removing groups, by deleting items within groups, and by copying items between groups. If, for instance, you often develop proposals, create a group called Proposals.

You could copy icons into this group for tools like Write, Calculator, and Calendar. You wouldn't be making multiple copies of each program using all your memory. Rather, you'd be making it possible to start these applications from within more than one window.

To start a program, all you do is open the window containing the program's icon, then select that icon.

Starting programs

An Exercise Using Program Manager

1. Make sure Program Manager is active.

2. Select New on the File menu.

3. Select Program Group.

4. The Program Group Properties dialog box opens. On the Description line, enter

   `Proposals`

   Select OK.

5. You'll now copy program items to your new group. Activate the Accessories group, which contains all the items you're going to copy.

6. Click on the Write icon, or move the highlight to it.

7. Pull down the File menu and select Copy. The Copy Program Item dialog box appears.

8. Select the group name Proposals on the To Group line.

9. The Proposals window is now active. Notice that it now contains the Write icon. Repeat exercise steps 5–8 for Calculator, Cardfile, and Calendar.

10. If you decide you don't need to access Cardfile while writing proposals, you can delete its icon. With the Proposals window active, highlight the Cardfile icon.

11. Pull down the File menu and select Delete. Confirm your choice. The Cardfile icon disappears.

12. To discover how easy it is to run programs from the active window, highlight the Write icon and press Enter or double-click on the icon. Write opens.

13. Close Write. If you want to exit Windows, just press Alt-F4.

Step 8
The File Manager

In this step you'll learn how to use File Manager. As its name suggests, this powerful tool greatly simplifies many file operations.

What File Manager Can Do

File Manager (see Figure 8.1) relies mainly on the actual names of files and directories rather than on icons, as Program Manager does. If you work frequently with particular directories, you may want to modify your default settings so that File Manager comes up when you start Windows, instead of Program Manager (see Step 20).

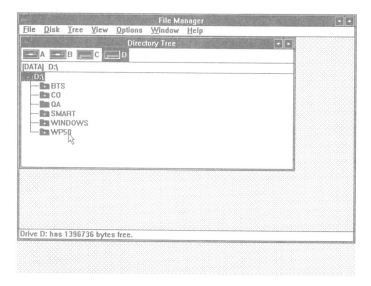

Figure 8.1: The File Manager

With this application, you can do much of the work possible with regular DOS commands—and it's much easier.

Working with File Manager

Looking through disk drives

Start File Manager by double-clicking on its icon, located in the Main program group of the Program Manager. You'll now see a Directory Tree, as shown in Figure 8.1. Several things you see here aren't found in other windows:

- Each available disk drive is indicated by a combination of a drive letter (for instance, *C*) and an icon identifying the type of drive (for example, floppy, hard, or CD-ROM).

- The disk volume label and directory path (in the figure, [DATA] and D:\) appear below the drive description.

- Each directory on your active (highlighted) disk is indicated by a directory icon appearing directly before its name. Thus, a combination of verbal and graphic cues shows you at a glance a drive's contents and structure.

To change to another drive, you need only select another drive letter. Then you can move down to the desired directory and select it.

Looking through directories

Once you are in the right disk drive, you'll usually want to skim the available directories. This is a fast operation.

A plus sign on a directory icon indicates that the directory has subdirectories. Selecting the icon reveals the subdirectory names, and the directory icon takes on a minus sign. You can reverse the action, making the subdirectory names disappear—the plus sign replaces the minus sign.

To see the files within a directory (or a subdirectory), you need only select its icon. An alphabetized list of files appears in the directory's window.

You can speed up your work by making several open directory windows visible on the screen at once—simply select Tile on the Window menu. Then move between windows as you like.

The directory window's View menu gives you the power to customize the way you skim your directories in several ways. You can, for example, choose to display any combination of file name, file size, and date and time when you last modified a file.

The View menu is also the tool to use for quickly arranging your files within windows according to their name, size, type (such as .EXE), or date.

Working with Files and Directories

You'll find it easy to do basic DOS operations with File Manager. In all cases, you highlight a file or directory and pull down the File menu. Then you can choose Create Directory within directories, or choose Rename, Copy, Move, or Delete commands for files and directories.

Most of these commands bring up a Confirm dialog box. If you like, you can turn off confirmation messages by issuing the Confirmation command on the Options menu. I'd be very cautious in doing this, however, because you can easily lose files that you want to keep.

Starting Programs

You'll often start programs by using File Manager. The most common technique is to open the appropriate directory window and double-click on the file name.

You can streamline this operation with the Associate command on the File menu. With this command you can start both an application and a document prepared with that application by double-clicking on the document name.

For starting frequently used programs, see Step 7.

An Exercise Using File Manager

1. Open File Manager from the Main group in Program Manager.

2. Move between your drive icons (A, B, C, D, etc.). You can use any one of the following techniques:

   • Click on the icons.

   • Press Tab to go to the icon area. Move the highlight box with the arrow keys, and press Enter.

   • Hold down Ctrl and press the letter of the drive you want to select.

   You'll find using the mouse the easiest way to maneuver in File Manager.

3. Double-click or use the arrow keys in combination with Enter to select a directory and view its contents.

4. Skim a directory's contents by clicking on the scroll bar or by using the arrow keys.

5. Pull down the View menu by clicking on View or by pressing Alt-V. By default, you see only the names of subdirectories and files, arranged alphabetically.

6. Select Details on the File menu. You now see much more information.

7. Go into the View menu again. This time select Sort By. Choose Size in the dialog box that appears. Your subdirectories and files are now arranged in order of their size.

8. Readjust the View settings as you want them.

9. Pull down the Window menu and select Tile. All the directory windows you've opened are now visible side by side. Select Cascade to see the windows stacked on top of one another.

10. Highlight any file and pull down the File menu. Select Copy. You see a dialog box asking where you want to copy this file. Cancel this operation.

11. Repeat step 10 with the Rename and Move commands.

12. Pull down the Disk menu and select Format Diskette. If you want to format a disk, insert one in a floppy drive and fill in the blanks in the dialog box. Otherwise, choose Cancel.

13. Close File Manager by selecting Exit on the File menu.

In this step, you'll learn about two Windows applications that can help you keep organized: the Clock and the Calendar. Clock displays the current time, and Calendar is a time scheduler.

What the Clock Can Do

Because Clock (see Figure 9.1) demands so little memory, you may want to have it displayed automatically when you start Windows—see Step 20 for information on how to do this. Then you can easily keep it in a corner of your screen, visible but out of the way.

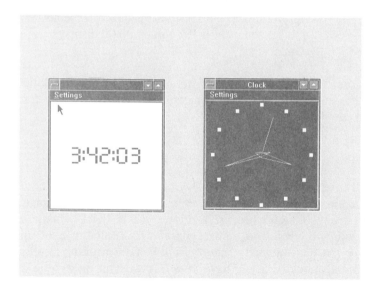

Figure 9.1: Clock's digital and analog modes

As Figure 9.1 shows, you can make the Clock show time in either digital or analog mode. In analog mode, the hour, minute, and second hands are displayed. Windows' clock is as accurate as your computer's internal clock, down to the second.

An Exercise Using Clock

1. Start Clock. The display is analog the first time you start the application.

2. Pull down the Settings menu.

3. Select the display mode (digital or analog) that is not currently displayed. The clock now looks different, although the time is still the same.

4. Open Clock's Control menu.

5. Select Minimize. The Clock is reduced to an icon in your screen's lower-left corner. It still displays the time.

You'll likely find the Clock icon easier to read in the digital mode. Remember also that maximizing another window conceals the Clock.

What the Calendar Can Do

You can set up Calendar (see Figure 9.2) to start automatically when Windows is started (see Step 20). Automatic starting is useful because it allows you to quickly organize your workday. The built-in alarm will remind you of appointments—a handy feature when you are working in other applications. You will have to decide whether these benefits justify the memory used.

The Calendar has an unchangeable display format. But you can switch between one-day and one-month views.

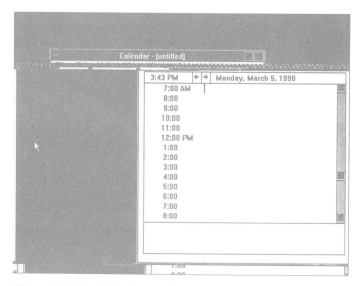

Figure 9.2: The Calendar in day view

Elements of the Calendar

The Calendar consists of appointment areas that display a view of either a 24-hour day or the days of the month, depending on which mode you've selected. In an appointment area, 14 entries can be displayed at once. With the default of 1-hour intervals between entries, 14 hours can be shown in an area at once. (You can change this default.)

Below the appointment area is a three-line scratch pad. (Each day has its own scratch pad.) In the day view, you can make a short entry next to the insertion bar. You can also scroll forward and backward through all 24 hours with the scroll bar or arrow keys. In the month view, you can highlight individual days. The work area contains one appointment area at a time.

The key functions of the Calendar are described in Table 9.1.

Key	Function
F4	Jump to a specified date
F5	Set or remove an alarm
F6	Turn on or off special day marker
F7	Insert or remove a special time in day view
F8	Switch to day view
F9	Switch to month view
Alt-A C	Set or cancel alarm beep or early alarm
Alt-A S	Set or clear alarm for appointment
Alt-E R	Remove all appointments between two dates
Alt-O D	Change defaults for day view
Alt-O M	Turn on or off special day marker
Alt-O S	Insert or remove a special time in day view
Alt-S D	Jump to a specified date
Alt-S N	Page to appointment area for next day
Alt-S P	Page to appointment area for previous day
Alt-S T	Display current day
Alt-V D	Switch to day view
Alt-V M	Switch to month view
Ctrl-PgDn	Page to appointment area for next day
Ctrl-PgUp	Page to appointment area for previous day
Tab	Switch insertion point between appointment area and scratch pad

Table 9.1: Key Functions in Calendar

To page through appointment areas, first place the insertion point in an area by clicking with the mouse or by pressing Tab.

To select day view from month view, put the insertion point over the date and press Enter. Regardless of the view representation, you can highlight the day currently being edited by pressing F6.

You can enter as many alarm times in the appointment areas as you want by pressing F5. The title bar or the Calendar icon will blink at the times you've set. If Calendar is active, a signal sounds, which you can turn off by selecting the appropriate option in the dialog box that pops up.

Tips for Using Calendar

If you share a PC with coworkers or your PC is networked, a personal calendar should be kept for each person. These calendars can be displayed next to one another in separate Calendar windows to help you keep track of them.

You can also create a centralized calendar, transferring important appointments from personal calendars via the Clipboard. (The Clipboard is a temporary storage area that you use when you move data from one window to another.)

At the beginning of the year, a work calendar for your whole company can be distributed as a Windows Calendar file, in which holidays and important company appointments have already been entered.

Each appointment line in the Calendar can hold 80 characters, 31 of which are visible at one time. If you have to write more, you can do one of the following:

- Use the scratch pad at the bottom of the window.
- Create another line using the Add Special Times command.
- Refer to a Notepad file containing more details.

Don't feel crowded by the day-view default of 1-hour intervals—just use the Add Special Times command to enter appointments for any time.

House-keeping

Files created with Calendar receive the extension .CAL. Since these files can get quite large if unpruned, you should periodically remove elapsed appointments using the Remove option on the Edit menu.

Alarm options

The alarm blinks to alert you about an appointment, even when the Calendar is an icon. You can also make it beep or have it go off several minutes before an appointment time.

An Exercise Using Calendar

1. Start Calendar.

2. Pull down the Show menu, and choose the Date option (or press F4).

3. Type the date **1/21/91**. Press Enter.

4. Pull down the Options menu, and choose the Day Settings option.

5. Leave the interval for the hour bar at 60 minutes.

6. Change the starting time to 6:00 AM. Confirm this entry by choosing OK or pressing Enter.

7. Choose the Special Time option on the Options menu (or press F7). Set this special time for 12:15 PM.

8. Your insertion point now rests on 12:15. Type

    Lunch at the lake

9. Set an alarm for this important appointment by pressing F5.

10. To make an additional entry next to 2:00, move the insertion point there by pressing ↓.

11. Type

    Call Freddy about contract

12. Set an alarm for this appointment.

13. Enter the following for 3:00:

    Tennis with Jerry, Bob, and Herb

14. To switch to the scratch pad, press Tab.

15. Type

    Yesterday's trip

16. Press Tab to leave the scratch pad.

17. Press F6 to mark this day.

18. In the Day Markings dialog box, check the box for Symbol 3 (o) by clicking on it or by pressing the spacebar. Confirm your choice.

19. To move back to the previous day, click on Left Arrow or press Ctrl-PgUp.

20. After 12:00, enter

    Flight from Denver

21. Go to the scratch pad once more by pressing Tab.

22. Type

    Take passport and draft of contract

23. To switch to the month view, double-click on the date or press Alt-V M or press F9.

24. Press F6 again so that you have two days in January specially highlighted.

25. In the Day Markings dialog box, select Symbol 3 again. You can see that the comments for the 20th are overlaid.

26. Switch back to the calendar area by pressing Tab.

27. Use → to go to the 21st.

28. Page to the next month by pressing PgDn.

29. Go to the 28th by pressing ↓, and mark this day with Symbol 3 by pressing F6.

30. Press Tab, and type the following in the scratch pad:

    Send in tax return

31. Press Tab again. Switch back to day view with the Enter key, and make this entry after 12:00 PM:

    Call tax consultant

32. Set an alarm for this appointment by pressing F5.

33. To set the early alarm, call up the Controls option in the Alarm menu by pressing Alt-A C. Enter **5**. The early alarm will go off at 11:55 AM.

34. Press Alt-F S, and save your calendar under the name APPTS.

35. Exit the application by pressing Alt-F4 or by double-clicking on the Control-menu box.

Step 10
Using the Notepad

In this step, you get acquainted with Notepad, the "little sister" of the Write application. Step 15, which covers Write, builds on what you learn here.

What Notepad Can Do

Notepad (see Figure 10.1) is intended for writing short amounts of text and provides no text-formatting functions other than word wrap. The files that you create in Notepad get the default extension .TXT.

Notepad is a convenient editor for writing and modifying system files, such as WIN.INI, AUTOEXEC.BAT, and CONFIG.SYS. These files can't be saved as formatted documents in the same way as word-processed files.

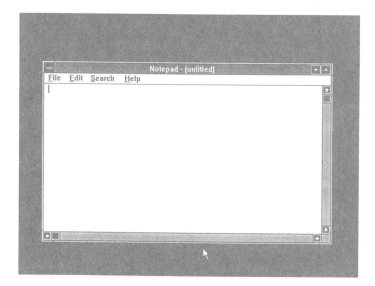

Figure 10.1: The Notepad application

You can also use Notepad to create personal notes and memos.

Menus   In addition to the Control menu and the standard File, Edit, and Help menus, Notepad has a Search menu.

Table 10.1 describes menu options and key functions in Notepad. If you have a mouse, click on the Edit, Help, or Search menu as indicated in the table.

Click	Press	Function
Edit, Time/Date	Alt-E D or F5	Insert time and date at the insertion point
Edit, Select All	Alt-E S	Select all text
Edit, Undo	Alt-E U or Alt-Backspace	Undo the last change
Edit, Word Wrap	Alt-E W	Turn on/off word wrap
Search, Find	Alt-S F	Input text, and search after pressing Enter
Search, Find, Match Upper/Lowercase	Alt-S F M	Match upper-case/lowercase in searching
Search, Find Next	Alt-S N or F3	Input a search string, then continue search
Help, About Notepad	Alt-H A	Display size of current file

Table 10.1: Mouse and Key Functions in Notepad

Working with Notepad

In Program Manager, you can double-click on the Accessories icon to open the window containing the Notepad icon. Double-click on the Notepad icon to start Notepad.

Opening Notepad

You can edit texts with up to 50,000 characters in Notepad. You can find out the number of characters in your current document by selecting the menu option About Notepad on the Help menu.

Size of files

You can page through text and position the insertion point by using the arrow keys, PgUp and PgDn, and Ctrl-Home or End, or by clicking in the scroll bar.

Paging

You can select parts of text by dragging the mouse pointer over the text or by pressing Shift in tandem with any of the cursor movement keys (↑, ↓, etc.). Choose the Select All command on the Edit menu (or press Alt-E S) to select *all* text in the document. Pressing an arrow key by itself cancels extended selections.

Selecting text

You can edit notes with the help of the Del key and the Backspace key. Pressing the Enter key starts a new line of text. Note that inserted text is not automatically wrapped; it goes off the edge of the screen. When you turn on word wrap, the horizontal arrows at the bottom of the document window disappear.

Editing notes

Inserting the time and date (press F5) makes it much easier to keep track of your notes and scraps of information.

Notepad has fixed tab stops that can't be altered. Press Tab to advance to the next tab stop and Backspace to go backward.

Tabs

To copy large text passages into Clipboard, select the text and then copy it by pressing Alt-E C (or press Ctrl-Ins). You can

Clipboard

paste the contents of Clipboard as often as you like into different places in the Notepad by using Shift-Ins. Or you can paste the contents into other Windows applications.

An Exercise Using Notepad

1. Start Notepad by opening the Accessories group in Program Manager and selecting Notepad.

2. Type the following text. Don't press Enter after each line.

   ```
   Notes from Dr. Calculus' Advanced
   Nuclear Math class, February 12. Topic:
   Fourteen theorems on the behavior of
   titanium alloys in the stratosphere.
   ```

3. The notes are hard to read because the lines extend beyond the right edge of the screen. Click on Word Wrap on the Edit menu (or press Alt-E W). All the words typed so far now appear within the window's borders. As you type more text, a word at the end of a line automatically drops to the next line.

4. The cursor now rests at the beginning of the document. For practice, check to make sure you've mentioned titanium. To search for the word, select Find on the Search menu (or press F3). Enter the word *titanium* in the dialog box. You then see the word highlighted in the Notepad window.

5. Press Ctrl-End to return to the end of the text.

6. Press Enter twice and then Tab twice. Type

   ```
   7.5 * 16 - 440 / 3.2
   ```

7. Press Enter twice and type

   The class couldn't solve

   Be sure to leave a space after *solve*.

8. Use the arrow keys to move the cursor to *7*.

9. Press Shift-End. The highlighting indicates that you've selected the line of arithmetic.

10. You want to copy the characters to another point in your document, not delete them, so click on Copy on the Edit menu (or press Ctrl-Ins). Press any arrow key to unselect the characters.

11. Press Ctrl-End to return to the end of the document.

12. Click on Paste on the Edit menu (or press Alt-E P). The document now ends with the duplicated arithmetic.

13. Select Print on the File menu to print the document.

14. Select Save on the File menu to save the document. Enter the name NOTES in the Save As box. The window's title bar now shows NOTES.TXT.

15. Select Exit on the File menu to leave Notepad.

This step introduces you to the Calculator. You can use this application for simple, nonprofessional purposes or for heavy-duty scientific work. As with Clock and Calendar, you may want this application to be loaded automatically when you start Windows.

What the Calculator Can Do

Figures 11.1 and 11.2 show the two Calculator modes. The application comes up in standard mode, and you can switch to the professional-level, scientific mode. So you have two calculators in one.

Both Calculator modes offer a keyboard area, a display area, and the Edit, View, and Help menus.

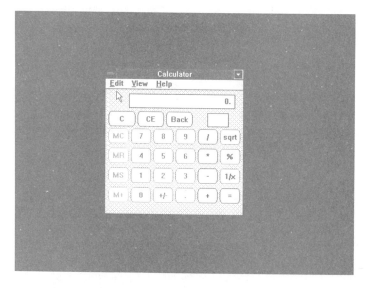

Figure 11.1: The standard calculator

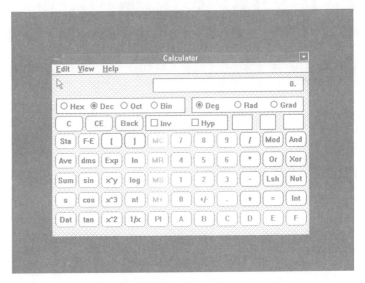

Figure 11.2: The scientific calculator

You can't change the size of the Calculator window. However, you can use either the mouse or the keyboard to move the window.

Working with the Standard Calculator

You can work with the mouse alone, if you like. Instead of using key combinations for certain functions, you'll find it easier to click on the respective on-screen keys.

However, you can enter numbers more quickly using your numeric keypad. Calculator will work with the numeric keypad only if you press the Num Lock key. When you leave Calculator, remember to unlock the keypad by pressing Num Lock again.

Table 11.1 shows most of the on-screen keys you can click on and the keyboard keys to press for the standard calculator.

Click	Press	Function
MC	Ctrl-C	Clear memory
MR	Ctrl-R	Display memory
M+	Ctrl-P	Add to memory
MS	Ctrl-M	Store in memory
+	+	Add
−	−	Subtract
*	*	Multiply
/	/	Divide
sqrt	@	Find a square root
%	%	Find a percentage
+ or −	F9	Change sign (+, −)
C	Esc	Clear calculator
CE	Del	Clear current entry
=	Enter or =	Calculate result

Table 11.1: Mouse and Key Functions in the Standard Calculator

Exercises Using the Standard Calculator

1. To practice using the basic functions, enter the following equation:

   2 * 3 + 3

   Press Enter. Your answer is 9.
   Now enter

   3 + 3 * 2

Multiplication and addition

Press Enter. This time your answer is 12. The Calculator pays no attention to the rule ''multiplication before addition''; it performs its calculations strictly in the order in which they are entered.

Percent-
ages

2. To practice finding a percentage, take 25% of 400. Enter

400 * 25%

Your answer is 100. Always multiply the number by the percentage, then press the Percent key.

Square
roots

3. To practice finding a square root, take the square root of 9. Type *9,* then *@* (or click on *sqrt).*

Your answer is 3. Since there is no square-root sign on your keyboard, the character @ is used as a function symbol.

Memory
functions

4. Finally, let's perform an exercise with the memory functions, using the same equation we entered before, 3 + 3 * 2.

Press 3, Ctrl-P (or click on M+) 3 * 2 Enter, Ctrl-P (or click on M+). You can see your result in memory by pressing Ctrl-R (or by clicking on MR).

Your answer is 9. This is a way to get a mathematically correct answer for the first exercise. Since the Calculator doesn't have a parentheses function, you can store intermediate results in memory.

Coordinating with Clipboard

The Windows approach makes a sophisticated double calculator very useful. You can pass input and results between Calculator and any other Windows application. For example, you could copy complex mathematical problems discussed in a document created in Microsoft Word for Windows into Calculator and pass the result back into Word.

An Exercise Using Notepad and Calculator

Sometimes it's a good idea to work out an equation in Notepad, then transfer it to Calculator.

1. Make sure that the applications Calculator and Notepad are both running in the work space.

2. Type the following equation in Notepad:

   `2.3 * 5.7 - 9.2 / 1.7`

3. Transfer this equation to the Clipboard: Pull down the Edit menu and choose Select All. Then select Cut on the Edit menu (or press Shift-Del).

4. Activate the Calculator window by clicking on it or by switching to it through the Control menu (or press Alt-spacebar).

5. Select Paste on the Edit menu (or press Ctrl-Ins). Calculator displays the result (*1.7*), which you can transfer back to Notepad via Clipboard.

The Scientific Calculator

Windows' scientific calculator has many powerful features, including

- Several numbering systems

- A statistical package

- Trigonometric functions

Because most of the mathematics involved in operating the scientific calculator lie beyond the scope of this book, I won't go into any examples.

Step 12
Using the Cardfile

This step introduces you to Cardfile, an electronic version of an index-card filing system. You'll learn to make efficient use of the special commands in this application.

What the Cardfile Can Do

Cardfile itself (see Figure 12.1) requires 54K of memory. Of course, the information you enter into Cardfile uses up more memory. Therefore, it's best to keep Cardfile resident in memory only when working with smaller cardfiles.

Memory require- ments

Cardfile is particularly suited to managing addresses, telephone numbers, and lists. It isn't possible to change or enhance its preset format for entering data—Cardfile isn't a

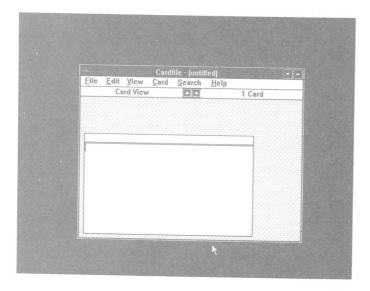

Figure 12.1: The Cardfile application

database system. You can, however, organize your entries by content.

Working with Cardfile

Opening Cardfile

You can open Cardfile by double-clicking on its icon within the Accessories group of Program Manager. You then see listed in the menu bar the File, Edit, View, Card, Search, and Help menus.

Paging

You can page through cards by using ↓, ↑, PgDn, and PgUp. The Ctrl key must be pressed in combination with the Home and End keys to select the first or last card in alphabetical order.

Using the mouse

With the mouse, you can click directly on the card you want to go to, or you can page through the cards by using the scroll bar. You can also select the index line to make a change by double-clicking on it.

Entering data

You use the keyboard to type in and edit the data in the information area of a card. Word wrap occurs automatically. You can move the insertion point with the spacebar, the arrow keys, the Ins key, and the Del key.

Files that you create in the Cardfile application get the extension .CRD.

Representing cards

In the Cardfile work area, you can either list the cards' index lines or display them on the screen as a series of overlapping cards. In the Card mode, only the first card is shown completely; the information areas for the other cards remain concealed. You manage the Cardfile cards just as you would cards in an ordinary roll cardfile. After you reach the last card, the first card reappears.

When you select List on the View menu, you display the index lines of your cards in a list format. The index line is the bar that appears at the top of each card, where you enter the text that Cardfile uses to alphabetically sort the cards. By choosing List, you can look through a large number of cards more quickly.

The menu commands and key functions of the Cardfile application are described in Table 12.1. If you have a mouse, click on menu choices (for example, click on File and Merge for Alt-F M).

Mouse and key functions

Click	Press	Function
File, Print	Alt-F P	Print the card in the foreground
File, Print All	Alt-F L	Print all cards
File, Merge	Alt-F M	Merge two cardfiles
Edit, Index	Alt-E I or F6	Input or change the index line
Edit, Restore	Alt-E R	Restore the previous state after a change
Edit, Text	Alt-E T	Switch to text mode
Edit, Picture	Alt-E P	Switch to picture mode
View, Card	Alt-V C	Switch to card representation
View, List	Alt-V L	Switch to list representation
Card, Add	Alt-C A or F7	Add a new card
Card, Delete	Alt-C D	Delete a card
Card, Duplicate	Alt-C P	Duplicate a card

Table 12.1: Mouse and Key Functions in Cardfile

Click	Press	Function
Card, Autodial	Alt-C T or F5	Auto-dial the telephone number on the index line
Search, Find	Alt-S F	Search for text
Search, Go To	Alt-S G or F4	Go to index entry
Search, Find Next	Alt-S N or F3	Find Next

Table 12.1: Mouse and Key Functions in Cardfile (cont.)

Tips for Using Cardfile

Interfacing with other applications

Cardfile's usefulness is increased by its ability to work in tandem with other Windows applications. You can transfer pictures from Paintbrush and other graphics programs, and text from Write, Notepad, and other writing applications, and file them in Cardfile.

If you plan to work for extended periods with a large number of Cardfile cards, you should switch the application window to full-screen representation or at least enlarge the window (as described in Step 5).

Cardfile files

For very large files that can be subdivided according to subject areas, you should open separate Cardfile files for each subject. If necessary, you can combine files into one cardfile by choosing the Merge option on the File menu. When using several different cardfiles, you should create an individual subdirectory for each.

If you frequently retrieve addresses from Cardfile, you should file the name and address information in the customary format in the first lines of the information area, the main part of the card that sits below the index line. This makes data retrieval considerably easier.

Elements of a Cardfile

For each cardfile, you create and store a file consisting of no more than eight characters and the automatically assigned extension .CRD. You can have only one file open at a time. It's possible, however, to have more than one copy of Cardfile on your screen, each displaying a different file.

Naming conventions

You create additional cardfiles with the option New on the File menu. Cardfile cards are automatically alphabetized by the entries on the index line. It's important, then, to choose index keywords carefully.

The information area, which is separated by a line from the index area, can accept text, pictures, or a mixture of both pasted from other Windows applications. You select the text or picture mode.

The index line can contain several keywords separated by spaces. The insertion point always appears in the information area when you open a card. You can move it to the index line using one of these techniques:

Typing keywords

- Double-click on it.
- Select the Index option on the Edit menu.
- Press F6.

You see a dialog box in which to type new text for the index line or to change old text.

When you type a telephone number on the index line, you should always include the necessary area code and prefix.

Telephone numbers

You can separate these with hyphens, for example, *212-555-6180*. You can use the Autodial option on the Card menu to automatically dial the number.

Transfer-ring data

The text on the index line and in the information area of a card can be freely edited. You can transfer data from the index line or the information area to Clipboard using the mouse or the keyboard. You can also transfer objects consisting of individual words and numbers from Clipboard back to both areas. Pictures and larger amounts of text can be transferred only to the information area, where there's enough room for them.

An Exercise Using Cardfile

1. Start Cardfile. An empty card appears on the screen.

2. Press F6, and type the following text on the index line:

   `Becker Thomas  Dr. 901-555-3167`

   Press Enter.

3. Type the following address in the information area:

   `Dr. Thomas Becker`
   `123 Garden Street`
   `Memphis, TN 38134`

4. Create a new card by pressing F7. Type the following on the index line:

   `Hill  Kay  B. 617-555-1319`

   Press Enter.

5. Type Hill's address in the information area:

   `Kay B. Hill`
   `412 Haven Lane`
   `Boston, MA 02118`

6. Create three more new cards for the following people:

   ```
   Michael Orton, 26 Prairie Lane
   Topeka, KS 66044
   913-555-2047

   Claude Hellman, 1243 Festival Street
   Annapolis, MD 21430
   301-555-2756

   Tim Hansen, 76 Freedom Way
   Portland, OR 97203
   503-555-1726
   ```

7. Duplicate the last card (for Hansen) by choosing Duplicate on the Card menu. Duplicating a card is useful when you want to retrieve the format of a card as a template—you simply type in the new data. To do this in one step, press Alt-C P.

8. Change the contents of the duplicated card. Press F6, and type the following on the index line (the old text is automatically deleted):

   ```
   Holmes   Ivan   505-555-6629
   ```

   Press Enter.

9. In the information area, you can select the old information you want to delete by simultaneously pressing the Shift key and the arrow keys, or by dragging the mouse. You can delete the selected area with the Delete key, but the area will be deleted automatically when you type new text.

10. Type the following in the information area:

    ```
    Ivan Holmes
    1419 College Lane
    Santa Fe, NM 80888
    ```

11. Page through the cards in your cardfile, using the keyboard or the mouse.

12. Switch to the list representation by pressing Alt-V L.

13. Search for Mr. Hellman's card: Press F3 and type his name as the text string.

14. Save your cardfile under the name ADDRLIST.

Using Control Panel

In this step you'll learn how to use Control Panel. This application lets you make decisions about how your hardware and
software run.

What Control Panel Can Do

Using Control Panel (see Figure 13.1), you can easily make
systemwide adjustments to settings like your cursor blinking
speed, screen colors, and keyboard layout, otherwise possible
only with an expert command of DOS.

The Control Panel window contains up to 12 icons, depending on your hardware and connections. These icons are Color,
Date/Time, Desktop, Fonts, International, Keyboard, Mouse,

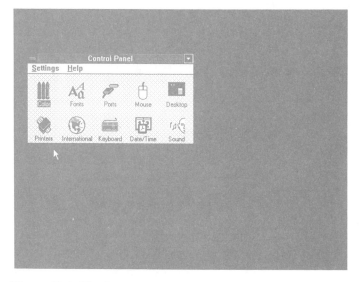

Figure 13.1: The Control Panel

Network, Ports, Printers, Sound, and 386 Enhanced. They can't be copied or deleted, since they represent functions of Program Manager.

Working with Control Panel

The following discussion of three of these icons illustrates how easy it is to make systemwide changes.

Color

When you select the Color icon, the Color dialog box appears. You can observe how default colors change as you enter new choices. To examine hundreds of personal variations, you can select the Color Palette option. If you have a color monitor, choosing this option produces the elaborate dialog box shown in Figure 13.2. If you have a monochrome monitor, you see fewer choices.

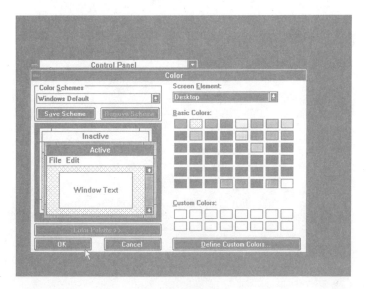

Figure 13.2: The Color Palette dialog box

If you'd like to decorate your desktop with patterns, you'll find interesting choices in the Desktop option.

Fonts

The visual display of characters on your screen or on the printed page depends in large part on the fonts you choose. Selecting the Fonts icon brings up a dialog box that shows both font names (with font sizes) and illustrations of approximately how the fonts will appear when printed. With this option you can either add or remove fonts.

Printers

The Printers option is Windows' tool for helping you set up your printers and select other printer options.

Installing printers

To install a new printer, you have to select the Add Printer option within Printers. The Printers dialog box then reveals a great deal of information about your installed printers, the default printer, and printers that you can install (see Figure 13.3). Proceed with the installation by selecting Install and following the directions in the new dialog box.

With the Printers option, you can also make choices about paper size, graphics resolution, printer cartridges, and network connections.

An Exercise Using Control Panel

1. Open Control Panel from the Main program group in Program Manager.

2. Select Color to open the Color dialog box.

3. The Color Schemes option is active. Review the effect of various schemes by clicking on the down button or by pressing ↓.

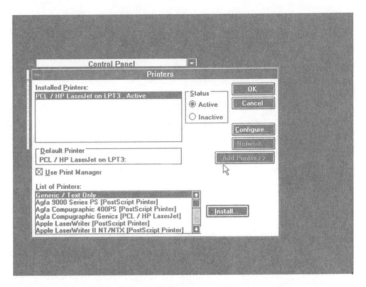

Figure 13.3: The Printers dialog box

4. Select the Color Palette option. If you have a color monitor, watch the screen coloring change as you choose different Basic Colors. You'll see different shadings on a monochrome monitor.

5. If you have a color monitor, select Define Custom Colors and experiment with different colors.

6. Close the Color menu.

7. Open the International dialog box. Review the various choices in the Language and the Keyboard Layout sections by clicking on the down buttons or by high-lighting the options with the arrow keys.

8. Pull down the Fonts menu. Notice how sample characters are displayed in the lower section of the window. Select a different font and observe the change in the sample. Select the font you want to use and close the menu.

9. Close the Control Panel by selecting Exit on the Settings menu.

Step 14
The Print Manager

15

In this step you'll learn how to streamline your printing by using Print Manager. This application increases your control over your computer during printing and your computer's efficiency.

What Print Manager Can Do

Print Manager (see Figure 14.1) allows the printing of many files to proceed out of view while you use your computer for other purposes. You can also step in to manage the printing of your files.

I'm assuming that you intend to print documents created within Windows applications. Although you can print from

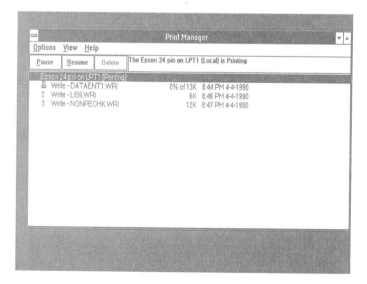

Figure 14.1: The Print Manager

non-Windows applications started in Windows, that kind of printing doesn't use Print Manager.

I'm also assuming that your computer is linked directly to your printer by a cable. Many of the options in Print Manager are different if your computer is connected to a printer through a network.

Working with Print Manager

From within Windows applications, you normally send files directly to the printer as you work. When you do this, Print Manager's icon appears at the bottom of the screen. It disappears when printing is complete.

You can keep sending files to the printer from various applications as you work. Each new printing job takes its place within Print Manager's list of jobs to do. This list is called the *queue.*

To take direct control of your printing, you have to move out of the application you are working in and open Print Manager. You don't have to worry about ruining your last printing request, since all the print information is safely stored in Print Manager.

When the Print Manager window appears, you see the kinds of information shown in Figure 14.1. The example shows the printer to which the printing requests have gone, whether the printer is currently printing, file names and sizes, when the files were sent, the order in which the files will be printed, and how much of each file has been printed so far.

You can do more than just read information, of course. You can, for instance, change the amount of information displayed on the Print Manager screen. You can select the Time/Date Sent and Print File Size choices on the View menu.

There are also more active ways to control printing. You can interrupt printing and restart it by selecting the Pause and Resume command buttons.

If you decide not to print a file, select it (if it hasn't yet started to print) and either click on the Delete button or press Alt-D.

Often you don't want files to print in the order you sent them to Print Manager. Altering this order is simple—select a file and either drag it to a new position or press Ctrl-↑or Ctrl-↓ to move the file and release the key.

You can also vary printing speed. The faster the printing, the more slowly your applications work. The Options menu has the choices Low, Medium, and High priority. If you want slow printing, select Low.

An Exercise Using Print Manager

Let's put three files in the print queue. Start with your printer turned off.

1. Start Notepad.

2. Pull down the File menu and select Open.

3. Open CONTROL.INI. Send it to the print queue by selecting File on the Print menu.

4. Repeat steps 2 and 3 with SYSTEM.INI and WIN.INI.

5. Close Notepad and open Print Manager.

Be ready to do steps 6–8 before turning on the printer.

6. Turn on your printer. Start printing by clicking on the Resume button or by pressing Alt-R.

7. Vary the printing speed by selecting different priorities (Low, Medium, or High) on the Options menu.

8. Delete WIN.INI from the queue either by clicking on the Delete button or by pressing Alt-D.

9. Close Print Manager.

Step 15

Using Write

You learned how to do some simple text processing with Note-pad in Step 10. In this step you learn to work with the much more powerful Write, a true word-processing application.

What Write Can Do

Write (see Figure 15.1) requires 223K of memory. Although it doesn't offer spell-checking, a thesaurus, columns, and many other features of large stand-alone word processors, it's surprisingly full-featured. Write works well for shorter professional documents, such as letters and short reports.

Windows' graphic orientation distinguishes Write from most other word processors. It can display text on the screen as it will appear when printed and can simultaneously represent

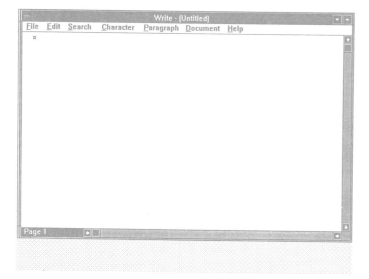

Figure 15.1: The Write application

different fonts, font styles, and font sizes. You can also use Write to transfer graphics from other Windows applications. Once these graphics are imported, you can change their size.

Files that are created with Write have the default extension .WRI.

Working with Write

Formatting documents

You establish overall format settings by choosing options on the Document and Paragraph menus. The Page Layout option on the Document menu, for example, sets such defaults as measurement system (inches or centimeters) and margins. You set tabs with the Tabs option. With Ruler you can use an on-screen ruler to make format changes.

While typing text, you usually format one paragraph at a time. Through the options on the Paragraph menu, you can set justification, line spacing, and indents. When you create a new paragraph, it automatically inherits the settings of the paragraph immediately preceding it.

Entering text

Write provides many features that make typing easy. The mouse moves the cursor as in other Windows applications. You can also use shortcut keystrokes to move the cursor quickly. Ctrl-→, for example, moves the cursor to the next word; Ctrl-End moves the cursor to the end of the document.

It's often useful to know where your pages break. The breaks show automatically when you select Repaginate on the File menu. Make sure that the Confirm Page Breaks dialog box doesn't contain an *X*.

You use options on the Character menu to control how your characters look. You can choose underlining, boldface, italics, subscripts and superscripts, typeface, and type size.

It's easy to make alterations in selected text. To select text, either point and drag, or hold down Shift while pressing an arrow key.

Write uses the left column of the work space as a selection column. Single-clicking on the selection column selects the line next to it, and double-clicking marks the paragraph to the right. When you single-click with the Ctrl key down, the sentence that has the cursor in it is selected. Pressing Delete erases the text.

You can also cut, copy, and move text using the options on the Edit menu. These three commands channel text through Clipboard. They're useful in moving and copying longer passages within a document and between documents. Selecting Undo on the Edit menu (or pressing Alt-Backspace) cancels these commands.

An Exercise Using Write

1. Open the Accessories group in Program Manager.

2. Start Write. You see the open Write window shown in Figure 15.1.

3. Type the following three paragraphs:

   The Flimflam Corporation invites you to apply for a Flimcharge Card. Simply fill in the enclosed application form and send us $750 to cover mailing costs.

   Flimflam Corporation reserves all rights to sell your card to the highest bidder. The Corporation will in such a case notify you within six years of the sale.

   This fantastic offer is valid through the next Friday the 13th. Please return

```
the form. And do not forget your check
or cash.
```

4. Select Page Layout on the Document menu.

5. Change the page layout to Measurements: cm, Left Margin: 3 cm, and Right Margin: 3.34 cm.

6. Select the entire document.

7. Pull down the Paragraph menu. Choose the following settings for paragraph formatting: Justified, Double Space, and Indent First Line: 1 cm. If you want to use the mouse, you can use the formatting symbols on the ruler. Note that the left margin for the entire document is determined by the small point on the ruler, which is originally located under the triangular margin delimiter for the current paragraph.

8. With text still selected, choose the Centered option, and then change again to the Justified option.

9. Copy the marked text to Clipboard, and move the cursor to the bottom of the document.

10. Retrieve the text by choosing Paste on the Edit menu or by pressing Shift-Ins.

11. Switch the Write window to full-screen representation.

12. You now have two versions of the Flimflam message. Insert a page break (automatic new page) by pressing Ctrl-Enter.

13. Select Change on the Search menu to search for the term *Flimflam* without entering a changed term, and choose the option Find Next. Move the dialog box under the ruler.

14. Continue your search by pressing F3. When the message "Search complete" appears, confirm completion.

15. Type **Flimflam** as the next search string and **Flimflam** as the change instruction.

16. Choose Change, then Find. When the first occurrence is found, turn on the character styles Bold, Italics, and Underline by pressing F6, F7, and F8.

17. Choose Change, then Find again, press F6, F7, and F8 again, and repeat until the message "Search complete" appears.

18. Return to the beginning of the text, and select Header on the Document menu. Press Enter.

19. Select the Right option on the Header's Paragraph menu and the Insert Page # button in the Page Header dialog box.

20. Switch to the Write window by pressing Esc.

21. Select Paragraph Centered, and type the following:

   Test printout for Write

22. Switch back to the Page Header dialog box. Leave it by pressing Esc. The header displayed in the text disappears, because the header is not normally displayed in Write.

23. Select Repaginate on the File menu. The Confirm Page Breaks option in the displayed dialog box shouldn't be checked. Confirm your choice.

Finally, we want to look again at how to print a document. We will also insert text from Notepad in the document.

Printing text

An Exercise Using Notepad and Write

1. Switch to Program Manager, and start Notepad.

2. Type

   The Story of the Big Flimflam, by Pygmalion Jones.

3. Copy this text to Clipboard.

4. Switch back to the Write window, and position the insertion point at the beginning of the text. Press Enter twice and return the cursor to the top of the page.

5. Select Paste on the Edit menu or press Shift-Ins.

6. Select Print on the File menu.

7. Choose the Draft option in the dialog box that appears. Indicate that you want to print from page 1 to page 1. After you confirm your selections, page 1 begins to print.

8. Close Write by choosing Exit on the File menu. Save the file under the name FLIMFLAM.

Step 16

Using Paintbrush

In this step you learn about Paintbrush. You may find this painting program to be the most comprehensive and intricate application in the Windows package. It gives you numerous graphics tools not found in the other Windows applications.

What Paintbrush Can Do

Although you can create black-and-white drawings with Paintbrush (see Figure 16.1), I strongly recommend that you use color, especially if you have a color printer or are doing presentation graphics.

You'll also find a mouse to be a necessity if you intend to work with any speed and versatility. It's awkward but possible to use the keyboard. In place of clicking or double-clicking

Mouse and keyboard

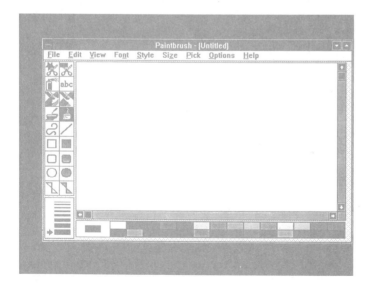

Figure 16.1: The Paintbrush application

the left mouse button, you press Ins or F9-Ins. In place of clicking or double-clicking the right mouse button, you press Del or F9-Del.

Graphics
limitations

Although you can create bar graphs and pie charts in Paintbrush, it doesn't automatically convert numerical data into business graphics.

Paintbrush doesn't support precise CAD/CAM drawings required by architects and engineers, nor does it offer graphics libraries. Windows does, however, have several files with the extension .BMP that can be brought into Paintbrush.

Files created in Paintbrush are given the default file extension .MSP.

Elements of Paintbrush

The Paintbrush screen has features you've seen in other Windows applications, as well as new ones. You are already familiar with the menu bar and the work space, referred to in Paintbrush as the drawing area. The cursor is also here, although its shape changes with its function.

Screen
areas

There are three new areas. The Toolbox, along the left side of the drawing area, provides several ways to draw and color pictures. The default tool is the Brush; you use it to draw lines. The Paint Roller fills enclosed shapes with solid color, Scissors cut out areas of the drawing area, Erasers erase, and Squares create square shapes.

The Linesize box in the lower-left corner of the window provides eight line widths. To change the color of your next operation, select a color from the Palette, at the bottom of your screen. On a monochrome monitor, you see fill patterns rather than colored rectangles.

Working with Paintbrush

Paintbrush accepts business graphics from programs like Microsoft Excel and text from the Write application, and then allows you to add freehand illustrations or to change various details. You can put this touched-up work back into other Windows applications, such as Cardfile and Write.

For detailed work, you can increase the size of any part of a drawing in Paintbrush. You can also decrease the size of a drawing, if you want to get an overview of a drawing that is larger than the Paintbrush window. In this mode, however, you can't edit your drawing.

Changing drawing size

For the most part, Paintbrush has the same possibilities as Write for altering the appearance of text characters, although their representation and arrangement in the menus is somewhat different. Because of the compatibility of the two applications, you can easily move documents back and forth between them. Paintbrush has character styles that Write does not have, such as Outline and Strikeout. If you move Paintbrush text into Write, however, you cannot edit it in Write because it is treated as a graphic.

Character styles

The Pick menu offers the commands Inverse, Shrink + Grow, Tilt, Clear, Flip Horizontal, and Flip Vertical, which have been specially designed for editing pictures.

Editing pictures

The Options menu helps you set such defaults as image attributes (for instance, the width and height of the drawing and the choice of color or black-and-white), brush shapes, an customized colors.

From the View menu, you can zoom in on all or part of a picture or use the Cursor Position option to help you align parts of a picture. You can also use this menu to turn off the Tools and Palette menus.

Zooming/ aligning

Resolution choices

When you print a sketch, you can choose from among several print qualities on the Print menu.

After working on a complicated drawing for some time, you may wish to undo several actions. Remember, however, that Undo stops working as soon as you choose a new tool.

Using Paintbrush's Tools

Choosing a tool

The easiest way to choose a tool is simply to click on it. You can also move to different areas of the screen by pressing Tab.

Drawing lines

To draw a straight line, select the Line tool and drag the mouse. When you use the Curve tool or any of the tools that draw irregular shapes, you have to click on several points in the drawing area. For example, you define a curve by clicking at the start point, dragging to the endpoint, and clicking at the apex.

Creating cutouts

With the Eraser or Color Eraser tool, you can define "cutout" sections of your drawing area. These cutouts can be cut, pasted, inverted, flipped horizontally or vertically, moved, etc.

An Exercise Using Paintbrush

1. Open the Accessories group in Program Manager.

2. Start Paintbrush.

3. Select the Brush tool.

4. Move the cursor into the drawing area.

5. Draw a simple freehand sketch of your choice, such as a flower. Make sure several parts of your sketch are totally closed up, with no gaps.

6. Move the cursor to the Palette. Select a new foreground color.

7. Return the cursor to the Toolbox and select the Paint Roller.

8. Click the cursor inside one of your enclosed shapes. The new color fills the shape.

9. Repeat steps 6–8 once.

10. Use the Text tool (the one showing *abc*) to type your name in the upper-right corner of the drawing area.

11. Select a new foreground color.

12. Use the Airbrush tool to spray several spots of color over your name.

13. Select Undo on the Edit menu or press Alt-Backspace to remove the spots from your name.

14. Close Paintbrush by selecting Exit on the File menu.

In this step you'll learn how to use Terminal to connect your computer to other computers.

What Terminal Can Do

Terminal (see Figure 17.1) is a full-featured telecommunications package that you use to communicate with other individuals, to exchange files with bulletin boards, and to receive information from commercial online services like CompuServe.

Windows' graphic interface simplifies procedures that non-experts, trying to use many other telecommunications products, find difficult to execute correctly.

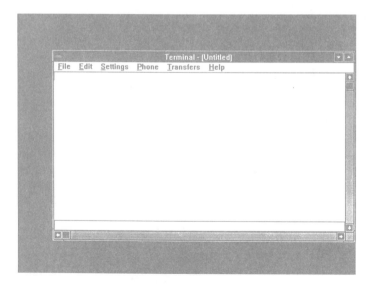

Figure 17.1: The Terminal application

You have only to give Terminal certain settings, and a telephone number is dialed, connections are made, data are sent from your computer, and data are received from the other computer.

To use Terminal, you must have

- A modem
- A free serial port on your computer
- A serial cable to connect your modem and port

Contact your computer dealer to make sure you have hardware that is compatible.

Elements of Telecommunication

Before working with Terminal, you must know important information about your computer system and the system you are connecting to, including modem type, baud rate, data bits, stop bits, parity, flow control, and terminal type.

Modems

Baud rate is a measure of the speed at which data is sent over the phone line. The higher the baud rate, the faster data are sent. The three most common rates for modems are 1200, 2400, and 9600 baud. All 1200- and 2400-baud modems are compatible with one another regardless of their manufacturer. If you try to connect to a 1200-baud modem from a 2400-baud modem, the 2400-baud modem automatically switches to 1200 baud. Unfortunately, 9600-baud modems are not as compatible—two separate standards exist, CCITT V.32 and V.29. Most modems that incorporate one of the 9600-baud schemes are compatible with lower-speed 1200- and 2400-baud modems, but the two standards are not compatible with each other.

Data bits

Data are sent to the modem in a series of ones and zeros. The number of *data bits* equals the number of ones and zeros in each discrete piece of data sent over the phone line. Both systems have to be using the same number of data bits. Your two choices are 7 bits—which is enough to represent all the letters of the alphabet, numbers, punctuation marks, and some special symbols—and 8 bits—which is large enough for the entire IBM PC character set. The most common setting is 8 data bits.

Parity is a rudimentary method of detecting errors in the data that are transmitted. By adding a one or a zero after the data, the total number of ones can be made an even or odd number. Your other choice for parity is None, which does not include a parity bit. The last two schemes, Mark and Space parity, are used less often. They set the parity bit to one or zero regardless of the data bits. No parity is the most common setting; you should use it unless you know that the parity of the other system is different.

Parity·

Flow control allows one system to temporarily stop another system from sending data. When you are using a modem, the only method that works is Xon/Xoff. Some systems do not support flow control, in which case you should select None.

Flow control

The *terminal type* tells Terminal what type of terminal to emulate. Terminals made by various manufacturers interpret codes transmitted to them to do such things as clear the screen or scroll a line of text. If you are connecting to another PC, you should select VT-100 (ANSI).

Terminal type

Working with Terminal

The first time you connect to a particular computer, you have to enter settings through the Settings menu. Then, using either these direct settings or a settings file, you place the call by selecting Dial on the Phone menu.

You don't have to retrace your steps every time you place a call. You can save your settings in a file bearing a .TRM extension. To use that saved file, you simply select Open on the File menu.

You send, receive, and review files by using the options on the Transfers menu. To save, delete, revise, and print the files, you use the File and Edit menus.

An Exercise Using Terminal

In this exercise you will create a settings file but won't actually place a call.

1. Open the Accessories group in Program Manager.

2. Start Terminal.

3. Select New on the File menu.

4. Pull down the Settings menu. Select the options and fill in the dialog boxes as described in steps 5–10. If a piece of information is already entered, don't change it.

5. Phone Number

   • Dial: 213 555 3827

6. Terminal Emulation

   • DEC VT-100 (ANSI): Confirm

7. Terminal Preferences

   • Terminal Modes: Line Wrap: Confirm
                     Sound: Confirm

   • CR-CR/LF: Inbound: Confirm

   • Columns: 80

   • Cursor: Underline
     Blink: Confirm

   • Terminal Font: System 10 point

   • Translation: None

- Show Scroll Bars: Confirm
- Buffer Lines: 100

8. Text Transfers
   - Flow Control: Standard Flow Control
   - Word Wrap: 79

9. Communications
   - Baud Rate: 2400
   - Data Bits: 8
   - Stop Bits: 1
   - Parity: None
   - Flow Control: Xon/Xoff
   - Connector: COM1

10. Modem Commands
    - Modem Defaults: Hayes

11. Save this settings file under the name SYBEX.

12. To place the call, you would select Dial on the Phone menu. Terminal would dial the number that you specified in the Phone Number dialog box.

Step 18

Using Recorder

In this step you'll learn how to use Recorder, the Windows application that lets you automatically execute a series of operations by pressing one key.

What Recorder Can Do

Recorder (see Figure 18.1) is Windows' application for creating macros. A *macro* is a series of actions that you record once and then replay as the need arises. The Recorder icon, appropriately, is a camcorder.

The obvious advantage of using Recorder is that you avoid having to enter the same key sequences over and over again; consequently, it will make your work more accurate. A macro

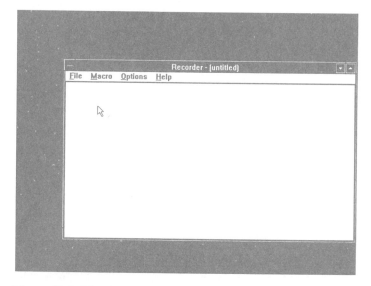

Figure 18.1: The Recorder application

can range from two or three keystrokes to a sequence of maneuvers that would fill a 64K file.

Working with Recorder

As you've seen by now, there are differences in the ways that
various Windows applications work. This means, for instance, that a series of keystrokes and mouse movements that
works fine in Notepad can produce totally unexpected results
in Paintbrush. So you need to decide whether a new macro
you create can work wherever you are in Windows or in just
one application.

If the macro will work only in a particular application, you
must first be in that application. And if the cursor is supposed
to be in a particular place within the window, you have to
make sure it's there.

Starting
Recorder

To start Recorder, you switch to Program Manager, open the
Accessories group, and double-click on the Recorder icon.

To record a macro, you pull down the Macro menu, choose
Record, and fill in the dialog box. Windows takes you back to
the original application window, where you can execute the
maneuvers to be recorded.

After you've finished recording, you can have the actions
take place automatically by using the signal keys you set up
in the Macro dialog box.

You'll discover that macros pay large dividends if you observe a few precautions.

You can use Ctrl, Alt, or Shift in combination with another
key to create a shortcut key. Be careful not to use a combination already used by Windows, such as Alt-F4, unless you

indeed wish to assign new functions to your basic keys. The Ctrl key is the safest key to choose.

Mouse movements don't physically work quite the same on different computers. I'd avoid putting mouse actions in macros, especially if you plan to use your macros on more than one computer.

You have a choice for how fast the macro should play back. Unless you want someone to be able to see the individual parts of the macro being executed, you should choose the Fast option.

Playback speed

Once you feel comfortable with the Recorder basics, experiment by putting macros within macros (called *nested* macros). You can always modify or delete macros.

An Exercise Using Recorder

You'll create a macro in this exercise that automatically gives you your heading setup whenever you write a memo in Write.

1. Start the Write application.

2. Switch to Program Manager and start Recorder from the Accessories group.

3. Select Record on the Macro menu. In the dialog box, enter the following settings:

    • Record Macro Name: Heading

    • Shortcut Key: Q

    • Ctrl: Confirm

    • Playback to: Same Application

    • Playback Speed: Fast

- Enable Shortcut Keys: Confirm

- Relative to: Window

4. Select Start. You're returned to your original Write window.

5. Type the following, using Tab or the spacebar so that entries typed to the right of the colons will be aligned:

```
To:
From:      [Your name]
Date:
Subject:
```

6. Press Ctrl-Break to suspend recording of the macro.

7. Select Save and choose OK in the dialog box.

8. Test your new macro. While still in Write, choose New on the File menu. Don't save your latest Write work. Press Ctrl-Q, the shortcut key you defined for the macro. Your heading is typed out automatically, ready for you to fill in details relevant to today's first memo.

Step 19

The PIF Editor

In this step you learn how to use the PIF Editor, a major tool for making non-Windows applications run the way you want them to run.

What PIF Editor Can Do

A PIF is a *program information file.* A PIF contains in-structions telling Windows how to run a non-Windows application.

With the PIF Editor, located in the Accessories program group (see Figure 19.1), you can create new PIF files and edit existing ones.

Figure 19.1: The PIF Editor

Windows can run almost any application, even those that don't have PIFs. But using a PIF gives you control over how the application runs. Windows creates a PIF automatically when you install a non-Windows application by using Setup.

Working with PIF Editor

*Creating
PIF files*

You control PIF Editor by making selections in three dialog boxes. In standard mode you see the dialog box shown in Figure 19.1. Let's look at some of your more important choices on this screen.

*Program
Filename*

Program Filename is the path name, or the route you take to start a program. If, for example, you start a file called Barfoog by entering BARFOOG.EXE in your C:\ directory, your Program Filename is

```
c:\barfoog.exe
```

*Window
Title*

The Window Title text box allows you to choose the identifying phrase that appears on an application's icon.

*Start-up
Directory*

The Start-up Directory text box allows you to enter the directory you want to be current when an application is started up. You could, for example, start in a word processor's directory that contains a particular kind of document.

Other settings on the PIF Editor screen determine memory requirements, what happens to a window when you leave an application, and special uses of shortcut keys.

In the Memory Requirements: KB Required text box, you specify how much conventional memory (in kilobytes) must be free before Windows can start the application. Leave this setting at 128 if you're unsure.

The XMS Memory line deals with extended memory. In the KB Required text box, you specify how much extended memory must be free before Windows can start the application. The KB Limit text box sets the maximum amount of extended memory that the application can use. For most applications you can leave these settings at the default of 0 kilobytes.

The Close Window on Exit option determines what you see on the screen after exiting an application. Select the check box if you want Windows to close the application and return you directly to Windows.

The Reserve Shortcut Keys section presents check boxes for five shortcut keys: Alt-Tab, Alt-Esc, Ctrl-Esc, PrtSc, and Alt-PrtSc. Windows normally reserves these shortcut keys for its own actions. Pressing Ctrl-Esc, for example, suspends an application and makes the Task List appear.

If Ctrl-Esc is also a shortcut key in an application, you may want it to work within the application rather than as a Windows shortcut key. To make this change, select the Ctrl-Esc check box. Note that this setting is in effect only when you run the particular application.

If you intend to run an application in 386 enhanced mode, pull down the Mode menu and select 386 Enhanced. You see the screen shown in Figure 19.2.

386 enhanced options

The major choices added here are Display Usage and Execution. For Display Usage, you can choose full-screen or windowed display; for Execution you can choose whether to suspend one application as you run another.

If you select the Advanced command, you see the screen shown in Figure 19.3. You find here more sophisticated 386 options for multitasking, memory usage, and display.

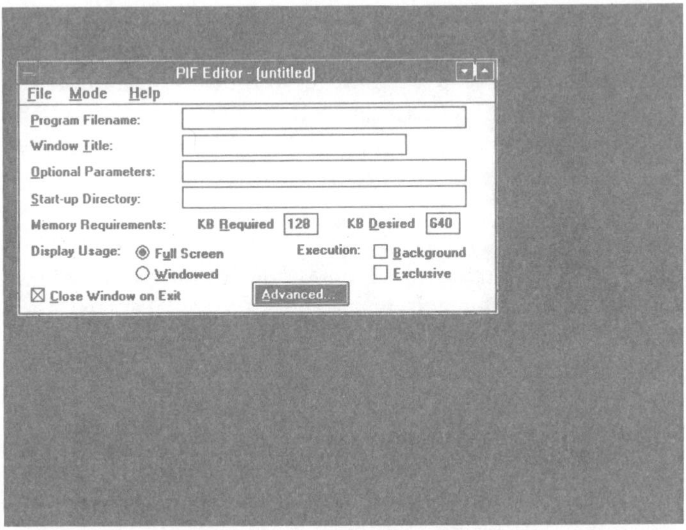

Figure 19.2: PIF Editor 386 enhanced mode

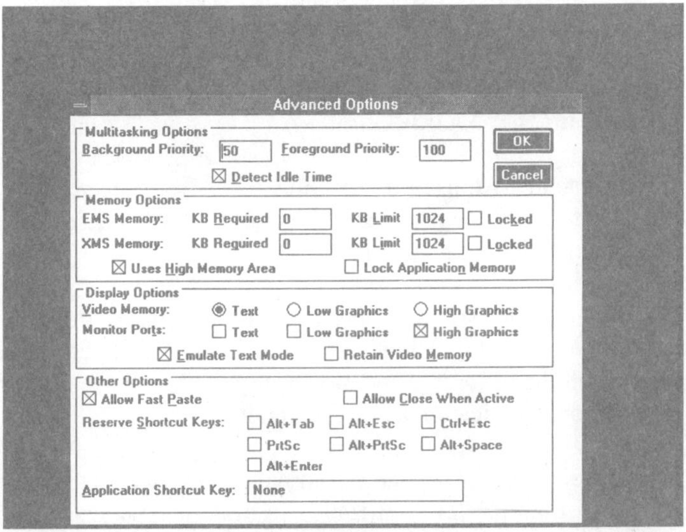

Figure 19.3: Advanced Options dialog box in 386 enhanced mode

Two areas on this screen contain particularly important options for determining how Windows runs in 386 enhanced mode. Let's look first at multitasking options.

When you multitask, you run more than one application at the same time. The active application is always in the foreground and others are in the background.

Multi-tasking

In selecting settings for Background Priority and Foreground Priority, you decide how much of your computer processor's time will be devoted to an application, relative to other applications that are running simultaneously. You can enter numbers from 0 to 10,000, although 50 is typical for Background and 100 is typical for Foreground.

For example, if you have two applications running, the one in the foreground might have Foreground priority set to 150, while the other might have Background Priority set to 50. The first application receives 75 percent of the processor's time, while 25 percent goes to the second application.

The Memory Options section is set up like the corresponding section on the standard-mode screen. The major addition is the EMS Memory line. Here you tell Windows the minimum and maximum number of kilobytes of expanded memory to provide the application.

An Exercise Using PIF Editor

1. Open the Accessories group in Program Manager.
2. Start PIF Editor by selecting its icon.
3. The Standard options dialog box (shown in Figure 19.1) appears if Windows is running in real or in standard mode. If Windows is running in 386 enhanced mode, you see the 386 Enhanced options dialog box

(see Figure 19.2). The settings go into effect automatically unless you change them.

4. Enter in the Program Filename text box the path name for your DOS file COMMAND.COM. If, for example, this file is located in the root directory on your C drive, type

   `c:\command.com`

5. Type the following in the Window Title text box:

   `Command`

6. Leave the other settings as they are.

7. Save the file by clicking on Save As on the File menu or by pressing Alt-F S. Name the file COMMAND.PIF.

8. Leave the PIF Editor by selecting Exit on the File menu.

Customizing

This step suggests more ways you can make Windows do what you want it to do.

Why Customize?

You can modify Windows in several ways to meet your needs. What are some reasons for customizing Windows?

- You find that some applications run too slowly.

- You frequently get a message about not having enough memory.

- The assortment of applications you normally work with has changed.

- You've added components to your computer and want to use them efficiently under Windows.

Let's look at some ways to change the way you start applications and handle memory.

Starting Applications Automatically

If you want a particular application to start automatically as soon as you start Windows, you have to change the command you enter to start Windows. In DOS, to start WordPerfect 5.0 automatically under Windows from drive C, you type this path name:

```
win c:\wp50\wp.exe
```

You can also open a specific document by using the same technique. To open, for example, a document named

LETTER1.DOC in WordPerfect, you simply append the document's name to the command:

```
win c:\wp50\wp.exe letter1.doc
```

To have Windows automatically start an application or open a particular document whenever you start Windows, you have to modify the WIN.INI file in your Windows directory. When Windows is started, this file tells Windows what applications to run.

It's a safe practice to copy WIN.INI under a different name before experimenting with it in order to avoid the risk of erasing the information in the file.

You can open WIN.INI in several ways. The fastest method is to use the File Manager (see Step 8).

When you open WIN.INI, you see these lines at the top of the file:

```
[windows]
load =
run =
```

Add to the run line

```
c:\wp50\wp.exe
```

Save the new version of WIN.INI. Now whenever you start Windows with a command line as simple as *win,* Windows automatically starts WordPerfect. You can list several applications (separated by spaces) and even individual documents on this line.

Another timesaving technique is to have the applications that you use most often loaded and available as icons as soon as Windows starts. You then merely have to activate the icon for the application you want to work in.

To set up Windows to do this, go again to the top lines of WIN.INI. This time add the names of applications on the load line.

You can carry automation a step further by modifying your system's AUTOEXEC.BAT file. (You can open this file from Notepad.) At the end of the file, type the usual Windows opening command line. If you normally start Windows by entering *win,* type exactly the same thing on the AUTO-EXEC.BAT line.

Modifying AUTO-EXEC.BAT

You can expand this command line so that WordPerfect is automatically started within Windows when you turn on your computer. Type

```
win c:\wp50\wp.exe
```

Working with Memory

As explained in Step 4, you can start Windows with different commands, such as *win/r* and *win/3,* depending on your system. But you can make more subtle changes, too.

One point to remember is that you have to balance priorities. For example, making every adjustment possible to speed up the operation of your computer and to run a number of applications demands a great deal of memory. If you constantly see an on-screen reminder of insufficient memory, you should balance your settings.

It's a good idea to have as much extended memory as possible. A very helpful utility included in your Windows package is HIMEM.SYS, a memory manager.

Extended memory

Look for a moment at your root directory (usually on the C drive). It contains the file CONFIG.SYS, which controls your system's basic settings. You want to be sure that one line of this file mentions HIMEM. You should see something like

```
device = c:\windows\himem.sys
```

You can make advanced adjustments to this line, but for now all you need to know is that HIMEM.SYS is working for you.

Swap files

If you are running Windows in 386 enhanced mode, your computer will slow down and give error messages as you get low on memory. An easy solution is to use a swap file.

A swap file reserves part of the space on your hard disk for use only by Windows. As you get low on memory, Windows shifts data from memory to this reserved area.

Although your swap file can be either permanent or temporary, I recommend setting up a permanent one if you have sufficient free disk space, because your computer will work much faster.

You may have created a permanent swap file using Setup when you installed Windows. You can check the Setup icon in the Program Manager's Main group to find out if you did.

If you don't have a permanent swap file, start Windows with *win/r* and run Swapfile with the Run command on Program Manager's File menu. Use the Swapfile dialog box to set the file's drive location and size.

SMARTDrive

You can also enter a line in CONFIG.SYS that instructs your system to use Windows' SMARTDrive, a disk-caching program that greatly increases the computer's speed but also uses a lot of memory. (See your Windows documentation for more information on SMARTDrive.)

Tips to Improve Performance

By now you know your way around Windows pretty well. Here are just a few of the many things you can do to further improve performance:

- Remove files you seldom use. Look especially at graphics files, such as those produced in Paintbrush, which typically are large.

- Save document files on additional disks.

- Remove the names of seldom-used applications from the load and run lines in the WIN.INI file.

- Avoid memory-resident programs, such as SideKick and PC Tools (although these work well under Windows). If you are in standard or 386 enhanced mode, you should run these programs as tasks from Windows, instead of running them before you start Windows.

- If you want to work with several programs at the same time under Windows, load the biggest program first.

- Periodically use a defragmentation program such as that found in Norton Utilities. After saving, erasing, and modifying files over a long period of time, portions of files end up scattered all over your disk. This fragmentation greatly slows your computer, because the disk drive's heads must find all the pieces of a file before doing anything with it. A defragmentation program rearranges the contents of the disk so that files are no longer broken up and your drive can work faster.

- Turn off the Spooler program in the WIN.INI file by changing the entry

```
spooler = yes
```

to

```
spooler = no
```

- Delete font styles (such as those in Write) that you don't use.
- Remove print drivers that you don't use.

Index